EMILY POHL-WEARY

GHOST SICK

a poetry of witness

EMILY POHL-WEARY

GHOST SICK

a poetry of witness

TIGHTROPE BOOKS

Tightrope Books
2 College Street, Unit 206-207
Toronto, Ontario. M5G 1K3
www.tightropebooks.com

Edited by Carolyn Smart
Typesetting by Dawn Kresan
Cover design by Deanna Janovski
Cover photograph by Rabin Ramah
Author photograph by Derek Wuenschirs

Printed and bound in Canada

We thank the Canada Council for the Arts and the Ontario Arts
Council for their support of our publishing program.

Library and Archives Canada Cataloguing in Publication

Pohl-Weary, Emily, author
        Ghost sick / Emily Pohl-Weary.

Poems.
ISBN 978-1-926639-82-6 (PBK.)

        I. Title.

PS8631.O35G46 2015   C811'.6   C2014-907859-5

I write these words to bear witness...
—*bell hooks*

Contents

III. True Contemplation Is Resistance

I

City Built by the Dead

I speak of the city built by the dead, inhabited by
their stern ghosts, ruled by their despotic memory,
the city I talk to when I talk to nobody, the city that
dictates these insomniac words…
　　　　—Octavio Paz

Ghost Days

After the shooting
I floated through life
ephemeral, near invisible

Walked into walls
slid under streetcars
became friends with Death

Called on willpower
to stop myself from fading away

Haunted friends
strangers who dared speak at me
smile, or even raise
their eyes to meet mine

Wailed and screamed
their happy little lives illusions
I had blood on my hands, our existence
constructed from violence and warfare

There is no sense in the death
of a young warrior or the rest of us
left behind, breathing
bitter air

World of Sorrow

Our frozen city celebrated
an immaculate birth
snow flaked from the sky
dusted icy pavement and hair

I stayed inside, warm, sipping wine
desperately hoping the boy I loved
would remain safe

Before that night
I had no way of comprehending
it only takes a second to tear
the spirit from a young body

Bullets
a .22 aimed behind parked cars
five blocks from our childhood home
business as usual ended a boy's life
nearly ripped a brother from mine

All the pretty ghetto girls
cried and puked vodka in the gutter
while their man-boys were shot like rabid dogs
family hopes bled onto grey concrete

My brother—
Why did you let the shooter
sit down at your table? Why did you drink
to blur right and wrong? Where did your world
of sorrow come from?

My brother—
Why did police shoot at your back
as you ran away?

What I Learned from the Newspaper

Someone I love was the intended target
of an attempted murder

Someone I love left a bar
because he thought the killer was gone

Someone I love was shot
in the arm during a rampage

Someone I love was involved in gang violence
which is what young, non-white people's deaths are often called

Someone I love's elbow was shattered
by a copper-jacketed projectile

Someone I love's best friend raised his arm
in self-defense, but it passed through into his chest anyhow

Someone I love's friend received two penetrating wounds
that travelled on a downward course into the abdomen

Someone I love ran home
after his friend was killed

Someone I love was afraid
the police would have kept him there to bleed out

Someone I love's premeditating shooter
used to be his good friend

Someone I love's girlfriend
is a bitch who better not snitch

Someone I love was terrified
to tell the truth in a court of law

That's what I read in the newspaper
but

Someone I love insists the boy who died
never carried a gun

Dreamer

Every sleep for a year began
like an action movie

I stopped full metal jackets
with bare hands
snatched my brother's shirt
as he tumbled over cliffs
leapt like Supergirl
into the path of speeding cars

They all ended in horror:
he died anyhow
slipped through my fingers
hurled his skinny brown body onto rocks
shot in the abdomen
smashed by a ton of steel
drugged in an alley
beaten with bats
left to bleed on the street

There was no sign of comfort
for so many days, no release of pressure
nothing to do but wait until he refused
to give into the numbness
and clawed his way back
from the edge

Vigilante Justice

Murder helped even me, a pacifist
understand an eye for an eye
the yearning to take other people's lives
into my own hands, guns blazing
posse popping bullets at my back

Vigilante justice
might bring my brother back from this nightmare
his nineteen-year-old girlfriend and their baby out of hiding
might restore the peace

Yet I lay immobile
night after night, pinned to the mattress
wondering if my personal ghost
also stalked the murderer's dreams
and whether his tiny son
cried for an absent papa

The spectre who visited
was familiar. He was famished
but had no mouth, thirsty
with no way to drink
he called for me to continue his martyr's journey
care for the boys left behind

To survive
I must remember a sweet blond boy
snatching birds and stars from the sky
before he could kill

I pictured his steady blue eyes
wished him strength and hoped for change

I prayed for peace
and I am not the praying kind
caught between one Jewish and one atheist parent
I prayed that this killer might become
the kind of man our dead friend
will never get the chance to be

Falling Angel

Our honey gigolo, golden, haloed, wary
Smiling at women, the boy who would kill

Carried disaster in the tilt of his chin
tightness of his shoulders, heavy droop of eyelids

He promised. He'd seen it all by twenty-three
couldn't fake forgiveness anymore

What remained was the scent of blood, a murdered friend
alcohol on the breath, perfect hair, a smeared newspaper photo

His glance spoke of a lifetime of loss
starting with his older sister, only protector

He was twelve, she a statistic
This city explained the nonsensical by calling her a whore

As if opening her legs was enough
to justify her murder

Some lives are worth collective mourning hymns
grief fuelled by outrage

Girls grow up to be warnings:
fear each other or die

Never Say Goodbye

for the forgotten girls

It's 1998.

If a fifteen-year-old girl
drinks in a parking lot at night
and a man comes along with a knife
how does the story end?

This time, she's with her best friend
windows rolled down
cool air clearing the smoke
because Sandy passed her driver's test
and Tammy scored some rock

Ordinary girls:
pretty, bold, skinny, whining
as they recover from a wild ride
think no one's around but scavengers

These two only ever wear crimson:
tank tops, miniskirts, jelly shoes
and the silence of their screams is so thick
it never exits raw throats

The world will forget tiny dreamers
smudged lipstick, thin necks
short lives past
vast expanse ahead

They giggle and bump
tobacco and weed makes their chests heave
we all know children get hurt
life is a process of hardening

They dance, laugh
about the good old days
a year ago. Shoot up, love the fire
racing through veins

Smear lamb's blood above the doors
so the murderer will pass over them
outside that industrial mall

Wrong place at the wrong time
says the politician

Clean it up, club zone, murder scene, pedophile
says the policeman

We know their mothers, brothers
boyfriends, best friends, neighbours
fathers, sons, enemies
grapple with what it means
to mourn the young
to have failed them

We can see the black Honda beater
being towed at dawn
to a police lot on the lakeshore

When you're a party girl
who bleeds scarlet or fuchsia
you believe the universe was created for you
you're a star that burns fear
and sometimes nothing exists but trouble

Don Jail

Murderer
Tossed in a box for my own good
Eight feet wide by eight feet long
The hole
Slit of a window, grey walls, beige ceiling
Tiles, linoleum
Pain from the beating
Bruised
Space to lie flat, barely
Pain
Alone
Jug-up!
Food? Shower. Alone
Turn around turn around turn around
Jump jump jump jump jump
Alone
Bible tossed in:
Abhor what is evil. Cling to what is good.
There are bones buried beneath the basement
Disturbed when they rebuilt the wing
Alone
Sleep, broken, alone
Is that mother? Sister? Friend?
With your shining faces
I'm so alone
Shit, push-ups, sit-ups
Sleep
Jug-up!

I eat, am hosed down, alone
Screaming
Where? Here!
Screaming
Alone, but not quiet
Screaming, weeping, lonely
For it all to stop
All of it: the nothingness
Nothing
Yard-up!
Outside for an hour
I feel the sun, but can't see it
Cement box, like that room
No roof
Back inside walls of grey, ceiling of beige, floor of grey and beige
Beige and grey, grey and beige, grey and beige, beige and grey
So afraid
Squares and rectangles close in
Walls move inward
Inward. Are they really moving?
Am I really alone?
Safe
Was I ever?
Jug-up!
Alone
Dizzy, panic, Bible:
Know ye that the unrighteous shall not inherit the kingdom of God?
Alone, along, alight, alright, a fight

Alone, a line, align, a life, line up for lines
A lifetime of alone
Speak to me, you were never here
Because I'm all alone
J. D. wuz here, he died alone
Jug-up!
Go on, go on, go on, go on, go on
Give up, give up, give up, give up
Stand up, stand up, stand up, stand up
Sit down, sit down, sit down, sit down
On, up, up, down
On, up, up, down
Jug up, jug down, yard up!
Yard down, count up, count down
Here fish, fishie, fishie, fish!
Big Al was here for 678 days
Al's one, alone
What was that noise?
I'm alone!
Again, alone!
A noise—there was a noise!
A snake—there was a snake!
Shit, I'm alone
Alone, shit in a hole
Wholly alone
Sit-ups, push-ups, jumping jacks
Forever and ever and ever ever ever
Aaaaaaaagh!

Aaaaaaaaaaaaaaagh!
Beating
Gone
I'm alone
Jug-up!
Help me Mama, help me sister, help me friend
I'm so alone
Ha! Alone! Ha ha ha ha! Alone
Sports Illustrated tossed into the room:
Colours, girls, sun shining, beach, waves
But I'm alone *Nor thieves, nor covetous, nor drunkards, shall inherit the kingdom of God.*
Fucking Bible
Yard-up! Raining
Outside, I walk alone
Alone, grey, wet, alone
Inside is beige, grey, beige, grey, beige, grey, beige
Hard, cold, hard, cold, hard, cold
Left to rot, ants eat my flesh
Down to the bone
That was a snake!
There's a snake in the room!
Snake, snake, snake! Snake! Snake! Snake!
No, I'm alone
Juan loved Sue in here, but I'm alone
Alone, alone, alone with the bones
Of a thousand men, dead beneath this floor
No boxes for bones
Jug-up!

Alone, I got a bone
Bones, boned, boner, bone, bones, bonnet
Ha, leave me to rot
I'm rotting alone
Leave me alone
Bible. Bible. Bible?
Fucking hell
When I get out I'll write my own book
For you. You, who put me in here
Boxed me up, all alone
I've still got two hands, two feet
Stomp on your face
Crush your skull
One day, I'll live for you!
I'll come for you!
But right now, I'm alone
Alone today, today alone
Alone
Alo…
A…
Jug-up!

This One's for the Ladies

Because at four in the morning
When the party's just getting started
All that exists is boys, somehow surviving
While us girls, left behind, hope for the best
Hold our breath, inhale as a collective
Use up everyone's oxygen

We wait, we wait, we wait
Sit on hands, painted nails bitten to the quick
Mop at cheap mascara and drown in firewater
Cry polluted rivers to clean these drugged streets
Watch television screens for signs of life

We pace avenues where men only
Spit, fight each other, love, scam
We mourn the ghosts who step from the shadows
Refuse to believe all that exists is murder and war
While the boys don't rat, stay strong
Get busy taking because they believe
No one gives it away for free

So this one's for my girls
Mothers, sisters, grandmothers
Morale boosters, baby mamas, nurses
Pole dancers who barricade their doors
To keep out drunken laughter
Call the cops, knowing they won't help
Say goodbye to men they love
When no other choice remains

We shield our lovers
Hold vigils, wail over 40-ouncers
Hide war resisters and defectors
Make the best stops on the Underground Railroad
Circle *la ronda* demanding to know about the disappeared
Put on our best black sashes to face off with tanks
Because all that worry needs to go somewhere
And caring can tear a person in half

My Epitaph Goes Here

Let 'er rip
My life was full
I told you I was sick
I was supposed to live to 102, and be shot by a jealous wife
I never killed a woman who did not need killing
A tisket, a tasket, my head is in the basket
I will not be right back after this message
I'm a woman cut in half in this world
Lenient to all errors except my own
I was killed by a taxi driven by Josephine Jacobs
I stepped on the gas instead of the brake
Two things I loved most: good horses and beautiful men
I hope they tan this hide of mine and make me into a man's riding saddle
I made an ash of myself
Steadfast in faith without intolerance
I was an exemplary wife and good mother, but a bad electrician
I am providence
Just sleeping
I am not really dead, do not believe these American lies
Behold I come quickly, thanks be to goddess
I have nothing further to say
That's all folks!

Call Me Crab Apple Girl

In memory of Ashley Smith, 1988-2007

Call me Ashley
No, call me Crab Apple Girl:
Thirteen, temper bouncing
Hard like round fruit.
They sail, those apples
I need to get the postman back
For stealing my neighbour's welfare money
Or not! Who cares?
It's only fruit

Sour little bombs
Could have been rocks
The postie wants to walk his path in peace
But I send him a clear message:
What he's doing is wrong
No one else has the guts, in this tiny town
I'm watching out for my neighbour

Bang! goes the judge's gavel
Shipped off to detention
Four months behind walls
Because of damn crab apples
And the teachers, they got into it, too
Saying I have troubles: fighting
At school, a temper, which we all know
My attention, I have none, it's a problem
Can't say I've learned my lesson in here

Breathe
Who cares!
This is a horrible place
I fight for food, air, fight for sense, to be alone
Fight the way the guards look through me
Fight the other inmates with their eyes
Learn hard and fast: it's a long, slow simmer
the fight must go underground when you're inside
Not the gasp of a girl with no air
Still, I rage

Months melt into years
I want to scream all the time
Period comes, a monthly punctuation
Laughing as chest blooms, hips widen
Food three times a day
I find small ways to remember I'm alive
Spit at their faces, claw at my arms, choke myself
Get thrown in the hole

Pinned
To an entomologist's spreading board
Cocooned butterfly in wrapping
I am no longer Ashley
I am pepper sprayed, battered
A girl with no name
No future
Oxygen fails
It fails

Jolt of a stun gun
Hooded, hog-tied, squashed
Duct-taped to benches at night
In the back of trucks as they take me
God knows where
Some new hell, jail

I'm injected in solitary
Permanent haze
The rooms are smaller than my parents' bed
I used to be a girl
A lifetime ago, I was a girl named Ashley
Who threw crab apples

Now I'm a lump of flesh
My life I no longer love
I rip strips of cloth from my clothes
Hoard my stringy instruments
Tighten ligatures around my neck
Tighter, tighter, tighter!
Lose sight in one eye

Laugh hysterically at the guards
Who can't keep their fingers off me
The bug they always grab from the left
So I won't see them coming
And move me in the middle of the night
Seventeen times in a year
I see the country from inside a hood
A cell, a truck, a cell, a truck

It's been four times four times four
Nighttime is a curse for the skank tank
That's when I pull the string around my neck
Tighter, so I can't scream
Can't piss them off

Guards care just enough
To beat me back to life
Always a new one, younger, harder
Some order that comes down the line
For stronger bug juice
Don't enter the cell if she's breathing
I know what that means
I am smarter and faster

In this system
There's no mother, no father
And no one's responsible
For a tiny little string
No more crab apple girl
No more caged-up Ashley
Think of me as free
Think of me

The Gentle Giant

In memory of George Wass, 1949-2011

How many candlelight vigils
will it take to light the sky
with grief?

One day, a person exists
in the room beside yours
the next, he's a "slow freak" captured
on paper above the fold: number six
while one, two, three, four, five
are still, amazingly, alive

He found peace
in the early morning, on a quiet street
smoked on the porch to welcome
the day, humming softly, and I swear
the birds sang just for him

Today, he's gone

I paint my face
with George's bruises
scream obscenities, find comfort in the voices
wear his tears, and pass the torch
to strangers

He was found mouth open
eyes wide, on the bathroom floor
in this ugly place

Coward
go pick on someone your own
size!

Nobody
has the right to take away
our freedom!

We'll be here, living
passing time keeping six and taking five
shouting four! or three's a crowd
as we two-time each other
when it should be
one for all

Those Who Died

After Ernesto Cardenal's poem "For Those Dead, Our Dead"

When you purchase new clothes
a shiny PlayStation, eat chips, take a walk, have sloppy sex
think of those who died.

When you're drunk at some house party
studying for school, working out at the gym
think of those who died.

When you've been on the sweetest date
feel loving and open
think of those who died.

When they congratulate you
as you make important decisions and soar in life
think of those who died.

When they give you unwanted privilege
treat you worse than shit
think of those who died.

When you're on stage, smiling into the camera, protesting,
making art, building houses, pushing paper, at the dentist
think of those who died.

They were addicted to chemicals
shot in the back, run over, stabbed, failed, hated
lost their teeth, the use of legs, voices, minds.

Wounded and angry
they fought, but were killed anyhow
tossed in graves with no tombstones.

Labeled psychotics, criminals, gang members, misfits
forgotten or simply never claimed
from the morgue.

Remember that you live where they did not.
You are the survivor and the advocate.
You must live for those who died.

II
You Will Fight and Fighting You Will Die

You will fight
and fighting, you will die. I will live
and living cry out until my voice is gone
to its hollow of earth
                    —Carolyn Forché

Gangland

We are the dealers
moving product fist over fist
breaking death in the concrete
cracks, shadows and corners
where we wait for knives
to stab us.

We are the managers
bigger, brighter, meaner
more resilient than you—
convinced our ladies believe
we are papa protection and they
deserve this hell.

We are the healers
smiling among you as we soothe pain
accept the lies, resilience abounds
tread lightly on the earth, become martyrs
make do, organize, socialize
try to ease the sorrow.

We are the lost children
minds like broken mirror
haunting grocery stores, swinging
from electrical wires, tripping through dirty lanes
in search of butts, belonging, and empty bottles
crying for all the wrongs.

We are the revolutionaries
young corner boys waging battles
forgetting why we fight in the first place
fake our way to the top, watch your back
then snatch the shoes off your feet
and take the socks as well.

We are the scammers
sliding credit cards from wallets
stealing identities along with wife, kids
and grass beneath your feet
cocking triggers just in case
you figure it out.

We are the copycats
slipping off treadmills and under streetcars
digesting television, magazines, billboards
yearning for romance, dancing around
wraith-like and famished as desires pile up
like mass graves.

We are the lovers
naked, eyes shut as we grasp for breasts
anyone's will do, we were torn away too soon
always want more, bigger, lovelier, rounder
we hope our Plexiglas good vibes will protect us
from the jealous in this sorry world.

We are the artists
refracting life, feeding it back abstracted
twisted to become more narrow, wide, lovely than before
you think you know, but can't even see
there's a certain truth only minds like
wet acrylic will ever understand.

We are the desperadoes
riding faithful steeds, playing the Pied Piper's flute
pistols popping, swords drawn in our wake
we disrupt the beat of a heart
with a smile, a wink, a touch
we know your secrets. They fuel us.

Some Girls

Some girls love hard fruit
can't pass a pregnant tree
without reaching stubby fingers upward
to pick bittersweet cherries
eat until their stomachs bloat and round

Some girls crave the cool skin of amphibians
root out creatures hiding at the bottom of lakes
hold them close to stay warm
convince themselves loving anything
is a kind of surrender

Some girls pass their days on display
in zoos and behind grocery store counters
scratch their armpits, look their best, smell pretty
throw peanuts and use tools like nobody's business
make the best advertisements

Some girls move continents away
wildest friends become gazelles
who dance along cliff edges
daring the world to catch them
burn fast and hot over campfires

Some girls dream of ravens
and hunt with wolves, take no prisoners
when they're near, tree leaves become feathers
raucous omens crowd the sun
mark the future for a love of carrion

Some girls slither fearlessly through grass
when they ought to curl into balls
coil inward, knowing predators will approach
strike out in pain, wait for the right instant
the perfect prey

Hungry Ghosts

The only way
I found to satiate grief
is kiss the cold, terrible places
expose fear and rage and lust
dance at midnight under the bridge
with junkies who need a piece
spin, smash cars, burn anything

Only one face shines
in the moonlight, howls
at the highway's wind

I change shapes
am ravenous and wanting
all I need is flesh

I hide in traffic
lie naked on pine needles
pound the cement and rubble
scrape at the bones of longing
gnaw at a cool mirage

Craft Supplies

a wise woman once told me
you can't expect miracles
from dollar store markers
though they're often realized
in the most unusual, tawdry places
like the bottom of a bin

stars and stickers are wonder
bought for the price of a pack of gum
stamps and stencils echo childhood longings
off-brand ketchup chips are shaped like hearts
non-permanent markers tattoo souls
hopes are coloured by number
people can be made cheaper, brighter, better
green turns gold after a brief while

be careful not to cut short your dreams
it's easier to trim and trim and trim
until there's nothing left but a stencil
a bag of coffee that tastes like dirt
paint that dries so hard, so fast
it smells of despair and aging
while lives in purples and oranges
march right on past

Fairy Tale

I

On the chewed-gum, bird-shit streets
he sings for his supper
because soup is filling, though the meat's a little chewy
and used to have a name

Animals in a neighbour's backyard
give cops a standing reason to search everyone's homes
an illegal rooster wakes him each morning
with its ca-roo, ca-roo-roo, ca-roo!

Rabbits burrow beneath shredded newspaper
squirrels cower in the tree branches
feral cats mewl at empty garbage pails that
raccoons have already picked through

II

By the time he is twelve
he has kissed so many frogs
turtles, snakes, rodents and puppies
not one of them is a prince

He survives anyhow, in this neighbourhood
where ladies of the night claim every corner
children go missing from behind swing sets
and holes in screen windows let other boys crawl through

At night our princess waits
for the world to stop turning, for him to grow big
he dreams of super-friends
and only cries out in his sleep

Finally he is old enough
to recreate himself as an Amazon
he steals a demi-god's lasso of truth
escapes in an invisible jet

But his father's rage will follow for the rest of his life
that voice in his head can break him
even on good days, and there are other days
when the air itself is angry

The Mirror Girls

High above the world
wind blows blue and cumulus white
tree branches smack the walls

What is this fort but safety
while boys yell from the ground
throw rocks, bottles

Once the ladder is up
nothing can touch the girls
only they exist, singing and whispering
crying into each other's mouths
as they pluck feathers from road-kill pigeons

We are doomed to live forever
her with the afro, burned shoulder, brown skin
me with the blonde ponytail, scarred wrists, blue eyes
whispering secrets into each other's mouths
working until our fingers are dead tired

We take our time
sift through nightmares, wander mazes
after midnight, descend to gather candle stubs
discarded by the Orthodox church
ask peacocks in the zoo to give us tail feathers
and seagulls for a gift of dander

It takes courage
yearn for the sun's warmth: melt wax, build wings
from the backs of a thousand city birds
plan to fly above it all, together
see the dirty lake extend forever from pavement
bikes tumble, cars crash, men fight
and sisters run with scissors in their backs

Cut Out Your Tongue!

Social worker, you awaken
bad memories as you make the rounds
of the community potluck
where food is a synonym for cardboard

Pretend to be one of us
but tread on the down-and-out
with shiny steel-toed combat boots
wave that white flag of research
invade personal space
call the police if anyone gets rowdy
in the quest to root out the reason behind my quiet
the meaning behind her tears

Ask questions that wouldn't be polite
in any other situation
especially the middle of a party
Have you ever suffered abuse?
Physical? Sexual? Mental?

You make me want to shove
a needle into my vein
and I don't have a drug problem

One man asks you to check off planetary abuse
because before you came along
he was sitting next to two pretty aliens
who shared his plastic flask

He tells you about his home world
where trees are made of happiness,
the soil is purple and water runs red
with the blood of a thousand nosy women

Sheltered

A heart beat in his palm
again and again and again
it was terrifying

So he threw it away
cracked and laughed like a rotten heart
fired dueling pistols into the air
again and again, hoping at least one bullet
would boomerang back to his heart

Donned epaulets
saluted the world with two middle fingers
then ran, ran, ran

Now it's not the repetition
or the constant change
but the fact it's forced on him
over and over

It's the dance, Mister, dance
and so many routines:
spaghetti on Monday
mac and cheese on Tuesday
burgers on Wednesday
tuna fish on Thursday
pizza on Friday
sandwiches on Saturday
chicken on Sunday

Move, Mister, move
up the stairs, across the hall, down the street
to a new roommate, social worker, friend, enemy
next town, next year, next time will be
tomorrow or the day after
right this second

Crawl, Mister, crawl
to dinner or your little room
roaches, mice, bedbugs wait for no man
and it's not over until someone else says
it's over

Ivy, Lichen, Moss

time seeps through the walls
covers the floors and windows with velvet
pins her down, despite a beating heart
it's all she can do to drag herself
across the living room carpet
hide in his warm shoulder
let the fog melt away

the sun blazes and flares
but it's not strong enough
to break through the haze

she'll do anything to be happy
change the plastic filter in her mind
dig a hole through the world
leave him behind, if she has to
paint the sky yellow and red and violet
or all the blues for a cloudless day
still the greens exist and nothing
can keep out grief for long

Take It Back

Hunting
for signs of life in the city
everything becomes a neon blur:
espresso, deadlines, traffic, wild boys
passion, insanity, resistance, sorrow

I crawl for the blue mountains
glaciers, rock, dirt
fall for the speed they move
relentlessly eroding

I need to stop
dreaming your nightmares
climb until my legs tremble
no longer hold me up

I don't love anyone
suck on ice
kiss tree trunks
inhale clean air
exhale your smoke, finally
I've been holding on so long

I go into town
make some guy really happy
lie in a field watching stars crawl past
smash around like a meteorite
etch myself into the earth's crust

I'm just a city girl
a blip with restless thoughts
deep secrets that equalize, tarnish
distract from the truth

There's nothing worse than putting in time
calling out at night
wanting it all

Our Heroin

"Every junkie's like a setting sun."
—Neil Young

She will smile until her cheeks ache
Stretch pennies into silver dollars
Trace the same small steps
Make up riddles to explain lies
Slink through shadowy places
Twist and spin and laugh
Until pavement wears down her heels

There's never enough time
Too many men with their fingers and leers
Life's a bowl of cherry bombs!

Scruffy chic allows the lady to hold her own
Men still throw money at her bloody feet
Addicts melt her on hot spoons
She'll take you down faster than any gun
Explode into shards of glass
With a wild holler of victory
Because poles gave her palms blisters
High heels burned her feet

In this world, there is so much wanting
And then there is always more

Dead Pig on Spadina

Thanks to Keith Henry, who contributed to an early draft

Sun shone on the captive's waxy skin
Pale and smooth as fine silk
His grin taunted a mad city
Bursting with gourmands and wanderers
Warmed by the knowledge
That the end is sweet and quick
It's the living that's painful
So over the shoulder went this giant beast
Hooves waving, ears flapping, tongue lolling
Freedom gone to market
To market went all the busy little people
The captor ran fast and awkward
With each heavy stride, he chanted:
Soup or sandwich! Soup or sandwich!
It's all good. The pig lived fat
So we can consume his flesh

Colour of Absence

During the decades Lydia went inside
she faded to a certain shade of beige:
hair, skin, clothes, words
all neutral

She frequently disappeared in a crowd
friends were shocked when she abandoned them
during a conversational pause
they took a sip of tea, glanced out the window

And Lydia was gone

She became confused:
people just weren't looking properly
she continued to sit in plain view

She could see them

Eventually,
she came to understand
the possibilities, and slipped away
only to see what would happen

Walked, invisible
through dirty streets
found comfort in the gaps
and crevices

Those years, there were so many close calls:
lights shone high on bridge railings
headlamps beckoned from oncoming traffic
LEDs bobbed at the back of bicycles weaving between cars

She got reckless
teased the meanest corner boys
scrawled angry slogans in wet pavement
chased down riot police
stored secrets in garbage cans
staged unseen protests
ripped up perfect lawns and planted weeds
only fell in love with exiles

Lydia was happiest
when she skipped over the gaping wounds
of a neighbourhood at war
crawled through abandoned buildings
swayed like tall grass
in a developer's empty lot

She dared the world
to stop moving, to really see change
knowing she was surrounded by followers
who only appeared solid and bright

Somewhere to Run From

It's not just a home, it's a house
where the head lingers, hearts crack,
past lives smile from every corner.
Could be up a tree, beside the tracks,
beneath a bridge, in a cardboard box,
the thirteenth floor, third door on the left,
white mansion in a field of grass.
Might make her hate your face, lips,
the green of a shirt. Could force her
to slide off your pants and scream
at the top of her lungs, eat a fourth helping,
puke, get drunk, piss on the stairs,
tear off her clothing, run outside screaming
until the sun ceases to shine, neighbours throw stones,
little birds careen for windows. Any windows.
Glass always shatters, mother always draws her roughly back inside.
So take shelter, love, terror, fear, nostalgia, lust.
Take it all in. Hard and hot.
Make the bed and do whatever causes the night
to press closer, squeeze her breaths together into strong wind.
Or else just remember that sighs still ache in her chest.
Will for the rest of her life
because kisses were snatched in every single closet
and the attic and the backyard. Matches sparked fires.
The television set was comfort.
She knows that nothing aches quite like the first stab.
No one hits harder than loved ones who betrayed
in dusty, half-forgotten ways.

Who weren't there or were there too much
or wanted something she could never give,
or listened wrong or not at all
or didn't want to part with a single piece.
Set whatever's there aside and picture a pretty girl
wandering alone at night, dreaming of a thousand lovers
and people she no longer knows,
has no interest in meeting again,
wishes hadn't set fingers on her long ago,
would blast through the heart if she could get away with it.
Gather those people in a room.
Give them a meal. Call it love.

Eyes Are Silent

After e.e. cummings's "somewhere i have never travelled,gladly beyond"

tourist in your land, i have travelled blindly
through war and fancy dances far from perfect homes
to hear a lifetime of morality tales marked by sorrow
much too deep and old, cackling like disturbed bones

you bring on with strong hands the rains
which expose my chill, scars and cravings
marked deep by hard silence
where the world is green, calm yet wild

a forest recovers, re-grows as the earth circles sun
desperate to understand our differences
like night and day, sun and moon, or why everything goes blank
when you are near, the sorrow clears away

your intense fragility pierces me
as if someone decided to lay bare dusty innards
make a martyr of dreams and terror, turn all that is fierce
into lust while the planet spins and voices drop away

i do not understand why you have this pull
nor do i trust the strength of gravity
there is need in the air and resistance in the bloodline
my life is richer than old growth because you are in it

Meaning

We are all holy
praying to aircrafts and satellites
because other galaxies are too far
and we are so scared

We are all un-whole
pretending nothing exists
except dollars, food and cunts

Words, bullets, needles, knives
slide too easily through flesh

We haunt the dead
simply because they beckon

Each person torn away too soon
takes with them some aspect of our selves,
leaves a need to fill

We wrap our holes in paper bags
and stow them on shelves
to gather dust

The older we get
the more we collect, the more we fail
people are lost and found and lost again
until loss is all that we are

III

True Contemplation Is Resistance

"True contemplation is resistance. And poetry
gazing at clouds is resistance, I found out in jail."
            —Ernesto Cardenal

The First Time

May 2003 was the first time
Toronto media became bloodhounds
and followed the boys around—
my baby brother and the others

Someone's little sister had disappeared
and the city shoved cameras and recorders in their faces
like rats hunting for dropped snacks

I wanted to smash everything
understood the desire to burn whole cities to the ground
change universes, professions, callings

Felt hatred for a group
that looks and acts like me—the writers, the reporters—
picking at the little bones for a good lead

Our universe really did become so narrow
justified following children around
hoping they'd let something slip
for the next big story

My brother's empathy
the most beautiful thing about him
wouldn't remain intact. And his friend
was navigating life without a little sister

How could any of these boys
possibly grow up to be good men?
Where would they put all their sweetness
when tragedy after tragedy after tragedy
bombarded them, so young?

Such a relief now
to know how much I underestimated resilience
the human spirit, healing strength of love
all that crap, clichés for good reasons

The boys' desire to thrive remained
but I never could stop the people, like me
who scavenged through pain

Wanderer

I felt every wind blow
You helped me breathe

While I did blind karaoke
You mouthed the wrong words

All the world cried for murder
So we danced against war

You terrified small children
I killed the young at heart

We stormed crumbling buildings
Called on wicked typhoons

I sucked face with hot pavement
You cooled me down with a hose

The neighbours called for a hanging
But we were never home

Sometimes space grows between two lovers
Patience helps the lost one find home

At Midnight

Last night I met a man with your smile

He said:
I am a ragged breath, a stutter
a bruise on skin so dark it barely shows
a split lip disguised by lipstick
a broken bottle with cigarette butts floating in dregs

I told him:
I can only ever see the places
my lover's already been
without him, small hills seem insurmountably steep

Recognizing the you in him
or the possibility of him on me
that drunk guy with your smile
he followed me home

I stuck to shadows
a whisper out of reach
swung my hips from side to side
stuck out my chest
sucked in my stomach

Later, as I hummed in bed
while you slept, oblivious, this stranger waited
down on the street, smiling up at our window
and called for a story

I silently obliged:
A father rages.
A boy suffers, cries, hates, fucks.
A girl is born.
Home exists, for a while.
A mother cowers, struggles, loves.
A wall rises and, eventually, falls.

He wanted me to join him
I understood that would make the man mine
but without cool midnight air
and the rest of you to go with it
there's no fun in that

Never Enough

I can't be the wife
you want me to be

So I put in curlers at night
scale the bedposts
scrape the bedroom wall
add notches to my belt
load my dueling pistols
cancel subscriptions
ignore the ringing phone
cry, view the world
through your window

You can't be the man
I want you to be
but love is there

Believe a Word

I want to murder something
If you're lucky it could be you
Believe me when I warn not to
Scream at the tin ceiling
Spin until you're dizzy
Rip a happy home apart
Kiss the soles of your dirty feet
Get the shakes for the right reasons
Just don't set the place on fire
Don't listen to my ramblings
I'm a mad woman and it's hot as hell
Everywhere, heat seeps from the cracks and holes
I'm going to burn tonight
Please pray for me, pray for rain

What Came Before

I miss the cigarette butts
and my best friend's fiery magnifying glass
slicing worms in the garden with a dirty shovel
waiting for the chance to practise on fingers

We hated all the boy smells
their tongues pressed against our lips at night
and words were shards

Dried-out pens captured city life
I wrote. I sang. I was an intrepid investigator
searching through crack houses
garbage dumps, back alleys, corner stores
threw ketchup at jumpers on a bridge
over a highway that kept away the lake
as angry young mothers in their prime hollered
out broken windows and tires beat the tracks
before the streetcars smoothed them out

She would hide in the bushes
practise dance routines to *Rocky Horror*
count the stars peeking through fog
refuse to come home until a truce was called

Later, in high school, I became a master of disguise
dated the quarterback, but never shaved my legs
smiled at the neo-Nazis, went home and protested war

I knew why girls at school turned up their noses
at the open wounds of a neighbourhood
where loyalty and love ran deeper
than anyone could bury

People Sleep Under the Bridge

Don't think we're all poor
though some of us are
don't think we're needy
though some of us are that, too

We have too much pride to fake it
get ego beaten out of us young
work hard or hardly work
live large or humbly
drink ourselves to stupors
savour a single glass

We're crafty and resourceful
small minded and spiteful:
pasty white bird ladies, purple Jesuses with dark brown skin
human cannonballs in pink spandex

We run convenience stores
but don't own them
or go to universities
and one day might run the schools
stock shelves and steal from the stores
bruise and anger, just like you

We are nomads and homebodies
survive unscathed or get murdered
know the cameras on every corner
and places below the radar

I'm not asking you to kiss the ground
just don't spit in our faces

Spring Thaw

I've been up this way before:
an eagle's flight made me cry,
bright sky was too wide open,
silently reproachful.

Ice sheets were punctured by avalanche
Lilies, snow melted everywhere,
water-logged everything and elk were rutting,
damn it. The love musk nearly killed me.

It's all different now:
love is a tiny string
pulled taut across cultures,
continents and years of difference.

Incomprehensible divides
give the world its meaning.

I could cry again, just thinking about how
there is no bridge over these impasses.

I suppose that is your gift:
you were always able to reduce me to tears.

Except now, the glaciers have retreated slightly,
the sun is out and I make way for warmer weather,
watch mustangs drink from spring ponds,
brown bears search for berries.

Do animals suffer too, when they're apart,
even if they understand that separation?

My Bang Bang Heart

The summer my parents destroyed everything
we pretended to be a normal family one last time
watched *Bonnie and Clyde* at the repertory cinema
then chugged home half-asleep in Dad's rusty blue car
divided and silent to find a skinny couple looting our house

Entered to the rustle of cans
clatter of drawers being pulled out
they'd come for me, I realized
someone heard the call
of my bang bang heart!

Father didn't notice my reaction
he never did, just grabbed my bantam bat
from the front hall and crept back outside
prowled through the darkness
while my mother, a tight-lipped firecracker
herded the pair into his backyard trap

It was late, but I could barely stand still
knowing Parker and Barrow had no reason to be there
except for me, they would find nothing of value
in our skeleton house, we were poor hippies
didn't own a television set, jewels, gold bars, cash
just a broken cassette player that ate every tape

Dad swooped in, brandishing the bat
cornered them from behind like that outlaw Jesse James
forced Clyde to grab some rusty fishing knife
that had scaled a thousand fish
but couldn't slice bread

I wanted to tell them I'd come willingly
they could take me now and leave unharmed
I stepped out from around Mother's legs
certain our kitchen held no mysteries
and saw it through their eyes:
a vault filled with treasure

Tell them why you picked our home! I hollered
but this woman was too plump to be Bonnie
and her man wasn't tall like Warren Beatty
she was already blasting our plaster ceiling
with a sawed-off shotgun, my parents flattened to the floor
I sighed and watched the couple flee

Confused, I ran for a window
pressed my nose to the glass
praying they would come back for me
hoping to catch one more glimpse of my future
I waited all night, listening
to the wily soundtrack of police sirens

Dad was red faced and shaking:
They could have grabbed you, held you hostage!
Why aren't you more like your brother
who understands how to behave and hid in the closet!

Our home bore those gunshots for a lifetime
after Dad left I understood that change
only happens when the head lets go

Hardly anyone answers the beat
of my heart's drum anymore

Lines About Emily

Emily is very rarely seen.
Emily hibernates in a cave.
Emily is pale in colour.
Emily mourns.
Emily doesn't like my commentary.
Emily makes silly faces.
Emily looks great in that dress.
Emily is gorgeous.
Emily is fat and ugly.
Emily loves the rotten ones.
Emily really likes dessert.
Emily needs to hear from you.
Emily is alone in a crowd.
Emily can't handle reality.
Emily isn't allowed in that neighbourhood.
Emily grew up there.
Emily will be dethroned.
Emily has a gift for that.
Emily lights up a room.
Emily isn't happy right now.
Emily is a secret.
Emily lives in exile.
Emily cries.
Emily wants what she cannot have.
Emily should just go ahead and take it.
Emily used to be a real girl.
Emily is the toughest person I know.
Emily is a tin soldier.
Emily holds me together.

Emily crumbles under pressure.
Emily can't keep up.
Emily is online again.
Emily has 1,500 emails in her inbox.
Emily has a new identity.
Emily shoots without thinking.
Emily kills for money.
Emily should hand over the gun.
Emily needs to be talked down. Again.
Emily is taking a nap.
Emily should get more exercise.
Emily skinned her knee.
Emily picks at scabs.
Emily oozes.
Emily wallows.
Emily dreams of mountains.
Emily is the vastness of sky.
Emily rides public transit instead.
Emily is a ball of anxiety.
Emily loves a graffiti-filled alley.
Emily wants to be Jane Goodall.
Emily ran away to live with the bears.
Emily can't stop.
Emily hasn't moved in days.
Emily plays too many video games.
Emily has a homing device for painful things.
Emily and I are definitely going to stay friends.
Emily and I just don't get along.
Emily is a teacher.

Emily is a writer.
Emily is a terrible friend.
Emily sings for her supper.
Emily lies and steals when she's desperate.
Emily comes from a long line of wanderers.
Emily spends too much time in her head.
Emily loses everything.
Emily wins, again.

Mountain of Bad

It's snowing inside this bus and you're out there somewhere, drunk or high, while I miserably flee a happy home, grateful I've had a bad day not a bad life, wondering what it would be like to be held by hands used for boxing and manual labour, the same ones that groped a woman who didn't want to be touched, got you kicked out of your last refuge, engulfed in the smell of tobacco, and I hope that snow crunches beneath your feet as you head for warmth, not some street corner with a steam vent—hey, do you own a winter coat, because all I ever saw you wear was a thick sweatshirt, which isn't nearly enough in a blizzard like this—and did you put your possessions in storage, if you have any stuff that matters or even a safe place to leave them, like those books I gave you that you'll likely never read, but I wrapped up and gave to you anyway, because I'm the kind of person who just can't give up, keeps hoping the twisting pain will ease and that the priest who abused you when you were a small child doesn't murder your dreams every single night, though I'm positive he does, and you still feel his hand on your thigh whenever a woman touches you down there, and I know maybe you won't be in contact ever again because I was the only person saying don't commit that robbery—it's definitely a step backward—don't drink that whole bottle because it rots your gut, don't smoke the weed and crack until you fall over—then again maybe there are half a dozen bleeding hearts like me who crave the way you make the world go silent, because you live like a mountain, with all the calmness at least on the surface, and time immemorial etched onto your skin, and those scars and valleys and forests that are so fascinating; but none of this matters if you don't have a bed tonight, even though you've managed to live long enough to get back on your feet a million times, and it's possible there's a loaded gun being held to your head in some pissy back alley, so I've been obsessively checking police reports for a murderer or corpse with your name, though you don't exist in that world of online data, and I probably annoyed you by saying try again, don't give up, there's more to you than that, real gangsters don't call themselves gangsters, and all the other stupid trite words I spat out on the off-chance something would sink in—who knows, it seems so dumb now, these would definitely be clichés if anyone else was saying them, but I mean every word, know you haven't always been a good person, that you've hurt others terribly, yet try to muddle through and give your kids the best life possible, despite the horrors and mistakes and haunting memories, we both know you've got to pick yourself up and try again or else life will mean nothing, to you or to me, so I sit here on this bus, shrieking your pain silently at the top of my lungs; it's bigger than this vehicle, leaks through the crack in the ceiling that's letting the snow inside and fills the universe with sharp needle-prick stars, a bright anger everyone in the world should see ricochets down the street, because it could be I'll never talk to you again, or else one day you'll be working on a road, hidden under a second skin of dust, grinning like some psychotic sun-stroked lover as if no time at all had passed, and I'll be cool and clean in my little hybrid car, desperately mouthing words through the window: you deserve better.

60 Reasons to Love Without Mercy

1. Cracks in the sidewalk could open at any time.
2. Fear will swallow you whole.
3. People are messy.
4. No one ever gets enough.
5. Hell is other people.
6. There is no hell.
7. Heaven is here on earth.
8. Most people work for an hourly wage.
9. Babies are born, after not even existing.
10. Broken hearts heal stronger.
11. Monsters exist.
12. Demons and angels are really just us.
13. Laws are broken every day.
14. There are no superheroes.
15. Addiction can make a villain out of anyone.
16. Shopping is addictive.
17. Most of us don't get rich or die trying.
18. Orangutans mourn their dead.
19. Elephants free their own from captivity.
20. Kindness.
21. Peer-pressure murders children.
22. It's not illegal yet.
23. Teenagers fuck in public.
24. Hearts grow tired.
25. Life is suffering.
26. Suffering is just part of life.
27. Other people are terrified, too.
28. Mercy will lead the good ones back.

29.   A single voice becomes your home.

30.   Windows are holes in walls.

31.   Strawberries are heart shaped.

32.   Most people don't want to make your life worse.

33.   There's a bit of old growth forest left.

34.   Hope.

35.   There are over 7,500 varieties of apples (if you count the genetically modified ones).

36.   Tomorrow's the same day all over again.

37.   Terror eases into relief…eventually.

38.   No one will berate you for doing it.

39.   Our bodies aren't strong: we're awfully fragile.

40.   No woman is an island.

41.   Men wear dresses.

42.   Free libraries.

43.   We all walk a hard path.

44.   Concrete and brick is dreary, but the graffiti artist always shows up.

45.   It can be more powerful than 1,000 orgasms.

46.   We are all just passing.

47.   Willows weep.

48.   Ghosts are usually dead friends.

49.   There are some evil spirits who keep busy.

50.   Cemeteries are great places to hold picnics.

51.   It's a form of protest.

52.   It's the most terrifying thing in the world.

53.   Inhibition is slow poison.

54.   Time passes quickly.

55. All you are is your stories.
56. Your story doesn't end until you let it.
57. There are magical sea creatures like tiny dragons, giant squid and jellyfish.
58. We're still alive.
59. We're zombies.
60. Nothing will ever be good enough.

Nothing Is Ever New or Good

when suddenly an alley
screams at me from behind bright murals
light bounces crookedly off a puddle
a shard of glass glints and the sun rips through fog
my lonely city is once again new and breathtaking
where moments ago there was desolation
water sluicing through dirty streets
around rubber boots and stilettos and worn car tires
and your shining brown eyes flash into my mind
white teeth tug at something deep inside
like my baby brother asleep in my arms
so long ago, now he's a man
or the hug you give me when I cry
fresh sheets on a bed as we break
skin against skin, fabric sliding up my legs
offering everything that you are, I am
a terrified purple flower struggling
through detritus and snow and the world
between us becomes so small, just a layer
of dust caught in a sunbeam or buttercup yellow
reflected on a girl's chin so that livid scar turns beautiful
heat climbs up me, rising through my knees
I'm writing a gorgeous sentence, perfect evocation
or riding my bike on cool nights
the rhythmic ka-thunk of your wheels
over tracks behind me, the smell of cherries in my mind
hiding in a musty cabin playing backgammon
as the rain falls into every crease and percussion drips from damp trees

because my brother and I used to fish off a dock
catch minnows and sunfish with a hook attached to a branch
and then there's play-fighting with Father at ten
him on his knees, pretending to swat like an angry bear
while we squeal happily and scramble around
or Mother and Grandmother chuckling together
at the table, forgetting their feuds for a second
so we catch the same laugh, fierceness, blue eyes
or joking with the beloved, fearsome boys who keep me safe
the stretch of stiff muscles after exercise
easing the sadness that gnaws deep inside my stomach
tea in the afternoon, the chaos of traffic
the cheese of Doritos on my first boyfriend's upper lip
a small parcel of food placed gently into my mouth
straightening your words, making them sing
as love surges painfully, inappropriately
for the survivors, dilettantes and murderers
who know the reason for a particular glance
an answer before the question's even asked
a conversation at midnight, being one step ahead
or the pain of my illness crashing sharply
raggedly against the backdrop of a familiar city
against the arms of my lover who pours water
for the first sharp coffee of the day
while airplanes fly overhead, off to adventures
I'm going too, just count the minutes:
home's a perpetual rumble in my chest

Listening to Animals

I know the frenzy
of a million panicked whales
clicking, groaning, screeching danger
while the ship's rudder churns close

Lone wolves pause to taunt me
realize I wander lonely too
and always mean that smile
veiled look of hunger

An understanding exists
between city and country birds:
we age like neurons firing
enjoy those wings today

Feral cats preen and wind plumply
despite the creaks and wheezes of an exhausted city
tufts of fur let go, force them to hunt in garbage cans
places they should never have to go

Again and again, coyotes laugh:
we are nothing if not space and time
bruises and scars and kindness
distance, such vast distance

I swing and listen
allow smells, sounds, movement to wash over me:
other planets are so far away, yet squirrels chitter
that I jump too quickly from tree limb to limb

Bears beg me to stop and lie around awhile
in the sun beneath airplanes
and fox wants me to sit, simply
because I sit so beautifully

You give up too soon, squeak the mice
who watch me on my back, staring up at the ceiling
imagining the specks are stars
hoping for a small piece of cheese

We're all in this together, chitter the roaches
with our riches and dreams and longings and rags
enough to clean a thousand floors
or bring home the ones we've lost

Fragile Peace

It's not that we forget or stop loving
we simply allow the dead to stop their perpetual wail
be silent for an hour, rest in peace

We learn to let fireworks
be fireworks on a perfect summer night, not explosions
that make us run through the list of who's been shot now

Nothing and no one dies
in the place where we store our losses
but the days become calm, muscles unclench
minutes pass without remembering a certain face
and trust opens its eyes again

Gaping holes fill differently
with ourselves, new people, hope—
plans for the future edge out the guilt
of not being there, caring enough, stopping the tragedy

We never cease to mourn
though it can feel like betrayal at times
we just give one hungry ghost
permission to eat its fill
and move along

The Word

This afternoon, I was reading my favourite book:
"Many years later, as he faced the firing squad, Colonel Aureliano
Buendia was to … " when the word

      "remember"

tumbled right off the page
and forced me to chase it around—
under the sofa cushions, through the legs of a chair
beneath a door, down the hall, into the kitchen
when it slipped below the refrigerator:

Tears on a teen boy's eyelashes, like stars only much closer
and her fists, always clenched, ready to fight the revolutionaries
or lovers who crowded her out of herself
All the times she longed for someone who didn't exist
The many dolls crafted from teeth, fingernails, hair
and breathed into life with repressed anger
All the wanting, all the waste, all the nothing
She stuck her fingers in so many boys' pies
ran naked through angry streets, lied like a trickster
took down names when strangers looked at her slant
stole candy and smashed windows
Bursting to speak, she stuffed her mouth
with pie and barbecue and sugar-butter
Took comfort from the knowledge that blood flowed out of her every second:
paper cuts, menstruation, ulcers, blisters and bullet holes
She peered at the world from beneath hooded eyelids

searched the shadows for friends
understood that wasted words caused girls with downcast eyes
scars, slit throats and boys who disappeared forever
fingers might tighten around her neck at any time

Now you know my story:
the bright laughter of grief has blasted my chest
too many times

Please take it, set it on a leaf, and let it drift away
in a river or the toilet: water rushes
but heals no wounds

" The world may be tiny but the heart's enormous."
—Shu Ting

Photograph by Rabin Ramah

Acknowledgements

Hugs and all the love it's possible to give to my family, for putting up with me no matter what.

Poet and editor Carolyn Smart repeatedly convinced me that these poems were worth sharing with the world.

Thanks to Jesse Hirsh, without whom these poems would not have been possible. Many more thanks are due to Alison MacDonald, Marge Piercy, Susan Musgrave, Cherie Dimaline, Karen Mclain, Irfan Ali, Chanelle Hanlan-Hudson, Sandra Kasturi, and Willow Dawson—all of whom read drafts of this manuscript.

Members of the Toronto Street Writers, Sagatay Men's Writing Group, Marge Piercy's Poetry Intensive, and the Banff Centre Writing with Style Program gave feedback on early drafts of certain poems.

Gratitude is also due to the Ontario Arts Council, *Arc Poetry Magazine*, *Descant Magazine*, Insomniac Press, Palimpsest Press and *Taddle Creek Magazine*, who supported me (and this manuscript) through the Writers' Reserve Grant.

"My Bang Bang Heart" (previously named "Bonnie and Clyde 1979)" was published in *Taddle Creek Magazine*, summer 2013.

"Dead Pig on Spadina" was published in *The Toronto Quarterly*, April 2011.

Author Biography

Ghost Sick is Emily Pohl-Weary's second collection of poetry and her seventh published book. Her most recent novel, *Not Your Ordinary Wolf Girl*, was called "a welcome twist on the paranormal genre" (*Quill & Quire*) and "a compelling, well-written story about growing up, artistic integrity and feminism" (*National Post*). Her previous books include a Hugo Award-winning biography, a female superhero anthology, two novels, and a series of girl pirate comics. Visit her at www.emilypohlweary.com